Watch Out, It's Poison Ivy!

MESSNER BOOKS BY PETER R. LIMBURG

Watch Out, It's Poison Ivy!
The Story of Corn

Watch Out, It's Poison Ivy!

by *PETER R. LIMBURG*

Photographs by the author

Drawings by HARIS PETIE

 JULIAN MESSNER   NEW YORK

Published by Julian Messner, a Division of Simon & Schuster, Inc.
1 West 39 Street, New York, N. Y. 10018. All rights reserved.

Printed in the United States of America
ISBN 0-671-32563-9 Cloth Trade
0-671-32564-7 MCE

Design by Marjorie Zaum

Library of Congress Cataloging in Publication Data

Limburg, Peter R.
   Watch out, it's poison ivy!

   SUMMARY: Describes the characteristics of poison
ivy and its relatives, poison oak and poison sumac,
discussing their effect on man and methods of treatment after exposure.
   1. Poison-ivy—Juvenile literature. [1. Poison
ivy] I. Petie, Haris, illus. II. Title.
SB618.P6L55   583'.28   72-11964
ISBN 0-671-32563-9
ISBN 0-671-32564-7 (lib. bdg.)

ACKNOWLEDGMENT

My thanks to Herbert L. Kraut, M.D.,
who was kind enough to read
and criticize portions of
the manuscript of this book.

Contents

1
Introducing
Poison Ivy

Each year, about two million Americans of all ages come down with a case of ivy poisoning. Although for some of them ivy poisoning is just an itchy, uncomfortable rash, others can become very sick and may even have to go to the hospital.

Poison ivy has been around for a long time, perhaps even before the first men came to America. Pioneer colonists from Europe learned about poison ivy the hard way—by getting it.

Over the years, frontiersmen and country

people gave poison ivy many nicknames, such as markweed, poison creeper, climbing sumac, three-leaved ivy, mercury, and picry. French-speaking Canadians called it *bois de puce,* or flea-wood, because of its itchy effect on the skin. But by any name, it's the same plant.

There have been many folk remedies for ivy poisoning. (A folk remedy is a cure invented by untrained people, or "just plain folks," instead of by medical experts.) Unfortunately, these folk remedies can be worthless, and some can even be harmful. Gunpowder, charcoal mixed with lard, iodine, coffee, cream, and even marshmallow fluff are a few of these cures.

Poison ivy belongs to the group of plants called *Anacardiaceae,* or the cashew family. The Latin name *Anacardiaceae,* which means "resembling a heart," was given by early botanists because they thought the fruit of the

Poison ivy, flourishing in woods and fields, was one of the hazards of pioneer life that early settlers in North America had to learn to cope with.

cashew tree looked like a bird's heart.

Botanists (plant scientists) decided that poison ivy was closely related to sumac, which also belongs to the cashew family, and so they gave poison ivy the scientific name *Rhus toxicodendron,* or poison–tree sumac.

Nowadays many botanists call poison ivy *Rhus radicans,* meaning root-forming sumac. This is a fitting name because poison ivy forms little roots along the sides of its stems which help it to cling to trees, rocks, and whatever else it climbs on.

Leaves in groups of three and climbing roots along the stem warn that this is a branch of poison ivy. Notice the different shapes that the leaves may take. On some plants, flowers and fruits provide additional clues.

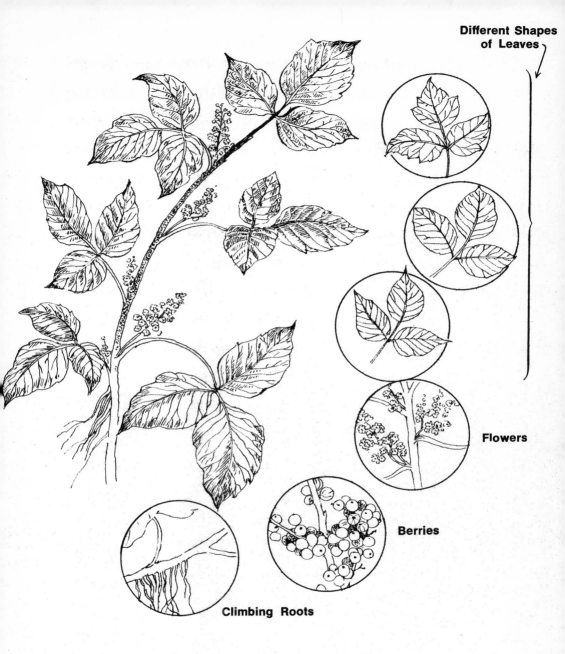

Different Shapes of Leaves

Flowers

Berries

Climbing Roots

WEST ROAD SCHOOL
PLEASANT VALLEY, N. Y.

Poison ivy is most dangerous when the leaves are on the plant, for it is the leaves that most people come into contact with. But every part of a poison ivy plant contains the poison all year round.

2
How to Recognize
Poison Ivy

Recognizing poison ivy can sometimes be difficult because it grows in different shapes. Usually it grows as a vine, but it can grow other ways as well.

Wherever there is something to cling to, poison ivy climbs. It climbs over any convenient object, holding fast with the rootlets that grow out of its stem. It sprawls over rocks in woods and fields. It climbs high up in trees and on telephone poles. It clambers along fences and stone walls, sometimes covering them entirely.

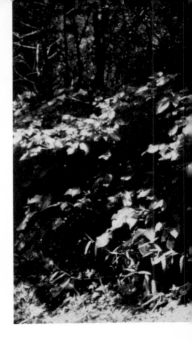

An old poison ivy vine twines around a hickory tree. Its branches spread outward, seeking sunlight.

Poison ivy covers a stone wall by a roadside with a lush growth of green leaves. This is not a good place to stop for a picnic!

Tree trunk or wire fence—poison ivy climbs both with ease. Leaves at lower left have been partly eaten by insects. At bottom of tree trunk is harmless Virginia creeper.

Poison ivy can also look like a bush. This happens when it grows up over a tree stump or a fence post, sending out branches on all sides.

Where there is nothing to climb on, the poison-ivy vines may sprawl along the ground, sending up many low stems loaded with leaves. People who do not recognize poison ivy may think that such a leafy patch is a nice place to sit. It is not!

Your Best Clue: The Leaves

There is an easy way to recognize poison ivy: *its leaves always grow in groups of three.* If growing conditions are good, the leaves can grow to be six inches long. But the leaves do not always look alike. They may be shiny or dull. They may be slender, or broad and stubby. Their edges may be smooth or toothed. Even leaves on the same

Smooth-edged and toothed leaves grow side by side in this poison ivy patch. All are equally poisonous.

poison ivy plant may look different. But they always come in threes.

"Fingers three, don't touch me," goes one version of an old folk rhyme. It is a handy way of remembering this warning sign.

A young poison ivy plant with smooth-edged leaves in a field. If left undisturbed, this plant could spread until it covered many square feet.

Deeply notched teeth mark the edges of the leaves of this poison ivy plant. In the background are grass and a young barberry bush (right).

Early in spring, the leaves of poison ivy begin to unfold. At first, the tiny leaflets are deep red and shiny. As they grow, they turn green and may lose their shine.

In summertime, the leaves may have

Poison ivy (left) growing next to a wild bramble, which has smaller leaves with many more teeth than poison ivy! If you will look closely, you will see warty growths on one poison ivy leaf. These are caused by insects that lay their eggs there.

small, reddish lumps on them. These lumps are growths that form around eggs that insects lay in the leaf tissues.

In the fall, the leaves of poison ivy turn brilliant shades of orange, red, and yellow. You may want to pick bunches of these beautiful leaves to take home for decoration. Don't do it! The leaves are still poisonous.

Flowers and Berries

Other clues by which you can recognize poison ivy are its flowers and berries. In early summer, clusters of small, greenish-white flowers appear on older poison-ivy plants. The flowers are followed by bunches of pale green berries that turn grayish-white as they ripen. In the fall, these grayish-white berries will

In center of picture is a cluster of poison ivy flowers. When polli- nated, the flowers will develop into berries about the size of a BB shot or match head.

A cluster of berries (center) hangs down from a bushy growth of poison ivy. Birds relish the grayish-white fruits and help to spread the seeds over wide areas.

help you to identify poison ivy, along with the leaves that grow in threes.

The Stems

Even in late fall and winter, when the leaves have fallen from the plants, you can still get a severe case of ivy poisoning if the stem of the plant breaks and the sap gets on your skin. This can easily happen when you are climbing on rocks where poison-ivy vines are growing.

Fortunately, you can often tell by looking at the stem whether a vine is poison ivy or not. As poison ivy plants get older, a fringe of coarse hairs sprout from each side of the

When leaves have fallen, poison ivy's hairy-looking stems are a tell-tale sign. Thick fringes of climbing roots give stems their hairy appearance.

stems. These hairs are really rootlets that hold the stems firmly in place when they climb rocks, trees, walls, and fences. No other vine commonly found in North America has this hairy appearance.

The poison-ivy plant can live for many years, and its main stem can grow more than two inches thick. A stem this size may look like a big, shaggy rope—but don't try to climb it.

A ropy tangle of poison ivy vines snakes over a stone wall, clinging by means of hairy climbing roots.

3
Where Does
Poison Ivy Grow?

Poison ivy seems to thrive in almost every kind of place. It grows in wet swamps and on dry, rocky hillsides. It grows in woods and in grassy fields, in wilderness and farmland. It even grows on city lots.

Poison ivy will grow where few other plants can survive. In moderate doses, even salt water, which kills most plants, does not seem to bother poison ivy. On a barren, sandy beach you may see poison ivy growing almost to the water's edge.

Poison ivy does not grow in California

A few feet from the edge of the sea, poison ivy grows on a sandy beach on Nantucket Island. It is not killed by the salt spray or occasional flooding by very high tides.

or Nevada. But outside of those states, the only places it doesn't grow are high up in the mountains and in the deserts.

Poison ivy's range stretches far beyond the borders of the United States. It reaches north into Canada for two hundred miles or more beyond the U.S.–Canadian border. And

The shaded area on the map shows where poison ivy occurs naturally. However, there are many local areas where poison ivy is not found.

it stretches south through Mexico to the Central American country of Guatemala. Poison ivy flourishes on the islands of Bermuda and the Bahamas, and is also found in Japan and Taiwan.

Fortunately, there are many parts of the world where poison ivy does not grow. It does not occur naturally in Europe, Africa, South America, or most of Asia, although people sometimes raise it as a house plant.

You are especially likely to run into poison ivy along fences, in the brush and weeds at the edge of a lawn or garden, and on the old stone walls that farmers used to build around their fields. In these places, people do not usually bother to clear away weeds and brush; so poison ivy has a good chance to take root and grow.

Another place to watch out for poison ivy is at the edge of a woods. Here there is plenty

*Bare for the winter,
stems and branches of
poison ivy stretch over
a stone wall. Unwary
people who climb here
may get ivy poisoning
if they break the vines
and get the sap on
their skin.*

of sunlight, which poison ivy needs, like all green plants. Deep in the woods, less sunlight gets through to the ground, and poison ivy does not grow as thickly as it does in the open.

4

What Makes
Poison Ivy Poisonous

For hundreds of years, people knew that touching poison ivy could give them an itchy, blistery rash, or worse, but no one knew why. Finally, in 1897, Dr. Franz Pfaff, a scientist at Harvard University discovered the poison. It is an oily substance found in every part of the poison-ivy plant: leaves, sap, roots, stems, flowers, and berries. It poisons people by causing an allergic reaction.

An allergic reaction occurs when the body's chemistry goes out of order. It starts when the body becomes sensitive to some outside substance, such as ragweed pollen, egg white, or the oily poison in the sap of poison ivy. Many of these substances are not harmful in themselves, but the body over-reacts to them, and this causes damage. Scientists are still not sure why the body suddenly loses its ability to react normally to these substances, but they know that it happens frequently.

When the body becomes sensitized to a substance, antibodies form in the bloodstream. Normally, antibodies help the body resist infection, but during an allergic reaction, they behave like war planes mistakenly dropping bombs on their own side. When the person comes into contact with the substance to which he is allergic, the antibodies in his blood combine with the outside substance. This sets off a chain reaction in his cells, causing them to produce a variety of harmful chemicals. These chemicals act on the body to produce the symptoms of the allergy, such as headaches, upset stomach, hives, stuffed-up nose, or rashes and blisters on the skin.

While all this is going on, the body produces other chemicals to neutralize the poisons. In this way, the body gradually heals itself.

About seven out of ten people are susceptible to ivy poisoning. (Susceptible means that they will be affected by the poison if it gets on their skin.) The other people are immune — that is, they are not affected by the poison. However, a person can lose his immunity at any time and become allergic to poison ivy without warning.

The poison is very powerful. Even one part of it mixed with a million parts of other substances will cause allergic reactions in some people. The poison lasts a long time, too.

Once a group of scientists at Cornell University cut some poison-ivy branches and spread them out on the roof of a shed. They left them there under the hot summer sun, in the rain, and in the freezing cold of winter. After eighteen months, the scientists took the dried-up poison ivy into the laboratory and tested it on volunteers. It was still poisonous!

5
Avoiding Exposure to Poison Ivy

If you are one of the seven people in ten who are susceptible to ivy poisoning, you will want to avoid getting it. The best way to do so is to learn to recognize the plant and not touch it. However, it is not always possible to avoid touching poison ivy, since you may not see it. The safest thing to do is to cover up your skin when you go anywhere that poison ivy may be growing.

For example, if you are going to hike in the woods, wear shoes and socks, long pants, and a long-sleeved shirt. If you are going to

Long Sleeves

Long Sleeves

Long Pants

Long Pants

Shoes

Socks

These two youngsters are properly dressed for a hike. Their clothing protects them against accidental contact with poison ivy.

work in a garden near poison ivy, wear gloves as well. After you come home, wash the clothes you have worn. That way no one will risk being exposed to any poison clinging to the clothes.

Some drug manufacturers market creams and lotions to put on your skin before you go out. These creams and lotions are supposed to act as barriers to keep the ivy poison from reaching your skin. However, they have not always been effective, and experts do not recommend them.

6

How You Get Ivy Poisoning

The most common way to get ivy poisoning is to touch the leaves with some part of your skin. The leaves contain microscopic canals filled with the oily poison, which is released at a very light touch. Of course, the harder you come in contact with the leaves, the more poison will be released.

You can also be poisoned by the stems or roots if they are broken and the sap gets onto your skin.

You may wonder how people can get near enough to the roots to be harmed. This

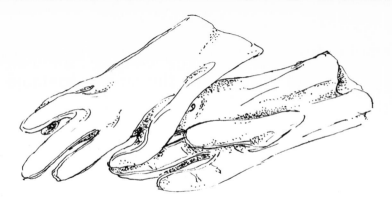

Susceptible persons may be poisoned by contaminated gloves or clothing.

can easily happen if they are digging in the ground near some poison ivy.

People who are very sensitive to the poison can get a case of ivy poisoning without coming near the plant. This happens when they pick up traces of the poison from tools or clothing that have been in contact with poison ivy. Even if the poison got on the tools or clothing months earlier, sensitive people could still be affected by it.

Others have been poisoned by the

smoke from brush piles on which poison ivy is being burned, for the smoke contains tiny, unburned particles of the poison. Fortunately, most people are not this sensitive.

Some extremely sensitive people claim to have been poisoned by simply walking near poison ivy when the wind was blowing in their direction. They believe that the wind picks up tiny droplets of the poison as it blows over the ivy's leaves and carries the droplets for some distance. Experts point out that this is not at all likely, since the poisonous oil does not evaporate into the air. They say that the victim's skin or clothing probably brushed against poison-ivy leaves that he didn't see.

Most animals are not affected by poison ivy. Dogs and cats can roll in it unharmed. However, some people become poisoned by stroking pets that have romped through poison ivy and have gotten the poisonous oil on their fur.

Cows, goats, sheep, and horses eat the leaves with no ill effects. Insects also feed on the leaves, and birds eat the berries without danger to themselves.

Pets that have been in poison ivy may transmit the poison to their owners.

7

What Can You Do In Case You Are Exposed to Poison Ivy?

You have learned what poison ivy looks like, so you will try to keep away from it. But sometimes poison ivy is hidden by other plants. Or for some other reason, you may not see the poison ivy until it is too late, and you have already brushed up against it. What can you do to keep from getting a case of ivy poisoning?

Washing with strong soap and water is one of the oldest and most effective preventive methods. If you are close to home, go into the house immediately and wash the part of your body that has been exposed to the poison. Strong laundry soap is the best, but if there is none available, use whatever soap there is. Wash thoroughly, working up lots of lather. Then rinse the soap off completely. Repeat this three or four times. This treatment is usually effective if you do it within a few minutes after you have touched the poison ivy. But don't wait too long. Even an hour gives the poison time to react on your skin.

Wash exposed areas of the skin thoroughly with soap and water. If done soon enough, this usually prevents ivy poisoning.

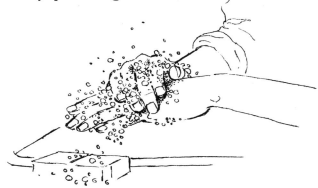

Another time-tested method is to wash the exposed part of your body with rubbing alcohol. The alcohol dissolves the oily poison, but you must remove the alcohol from your skin immediately, or it will spread the poison. Doctors recommend that you pat the alcohol dry with absorbent cotton or anything else that soaks up liquids quickly.

If your parents (or another adult) are home, tell them what has happened. They may want to supervise your treatment and make sure you do it thoroughly.

If you are on a hike or picnic, it is a good idea to carry a small piece of soap in your pocket or backpack in case of an emergency. Then you can wash the exposed area of your skin with water from your canteen or from a lake or stream if there is one nearby.

If you don't have soap and water handy, sometimes a natural remedy is available—

the juice of the jewelweed.

Jewelweed, or wild impatience, is a wild-flower with bright-colored orange blossoms. It grows in damp locations, often near poison ivy. It may be anywhere from a few inches to several feet tall. The stem of the jewelweed is very juicy, especially at the nodes (the

A natural remedy that helps some people is the juice of the jewelweed.

joints between the sections of the stem). Crush a jewelweed stem and rub plenty of the juice on the exposed area of your skin. In many cases, this remedy will prevent ivy poisoning.

Jewelweed has been used as a folk remedy for many years. Perhaps early settlers learned about it from the Indians, or perhaps they discovered its usefulness by accident. Whether the jewelweed juice washes away the poison or neutralizes it chemically is not known. But, like many folk remedies, it often works.

If your parents don't know about these preventive measures tell them. They are a good thing for everyone to know.

8
The Symptoms
of Ivy Poisoning

You have been on a long hike in the woods and had a wonderful time. A day or two later, a patch of skin on one of your arms breaks out in a red, itchy rash.

Could it be poison ivy? If you recognize the symptoms, or signs, of ivy poisoning, you will be able to tell whether the itch is caused by poison ivy. This will help you and your parents to know what to do about it.

The symptoms of ivy poisoning usually appear from 24 to 48 hours after you have been exposed. However, the time varies from person to person. The symptoms may appear within a few hours, or as long as a week later.

The first signs of ivy poisoning are itching and redness of the skin. The skin may also swell up, and sometimes have raised streaks. Next, little, fluid-filled blisters appear. The blisters often form straight, short rows. This is because of the way the poison is spread when the leaves brush along your skin.

In severe cases of ivy poisoning, the blisters grow quite large and may run together, forming giant blisters. They may become filled with pus caused by damage done to the skin tissues by the poison. The affected area may also become badly swollen.

People who are extremely sensitive to the poison may become very sick from it.

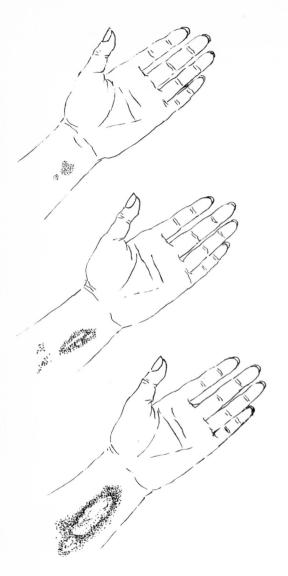

These drawings show stages in a case of ivy poisoning. Not all victims develop such large blisters, but some are even more badly affected.

They may run a fever, get swollen glands, and have muscle aches and pains—all this in addition to the discomfort of itching and swelling skin. They may even suffer damage to their kidneys. Fortunately, reactions as bad as these happen only to a few people.

Even when you break out with the symptoms, your body is fighting the poison. As the body develops its defenses, the blisters dry up, the swelling goes down and the itching gradually disappears. A mild case of ivy poisoning is usually over in one to two weeks. More severe cases last longer.

You cannot get ivy poisoning by touching the rash of another person. But when you have it yourself, your whole body becomes highly sensitive to the poisonous oil. If you scratch—or even touch—the affected area, your fingers can pick up tiny amounts of the poison remaining on your skin. If you then touch another part of your skin without first washing your hands, you can spread a new patch of poison on yourself.

Many people believe that the fluid inside the blisters is poisonous and can spread the rash if the blisters are broken. However, scientists have found that this is not so. The fluid in blisters is actually harmless. It is traces of the poison on your skin, or even under your fingernails, that do the harm.

9

How to Treat a Case of Ivy Poisoning

What can you do when the itching and the blisters of ivy poisoning appear? If you have a severe case, with bad swelling or big blisters, or if the poison has spread to your eyes, SEE A DOCTOR AT ONCE. DO NOT TRY TO TREAT THE POISONING AT HOME.

But, if you have a mild case, there are a number of things that can be done to relieve the symptoms. One good method for relieving the itching is to turn on the cold-water tap and let cold water run over the affected area for a few minutes. This treatment works by temporarily "knocking out" the nerve endings in the outer layer of your skin. These nerve endings are the ones that transmit the sensation of itching to your brain. When they are prevented from sending signals to the brain, you do not feel the itch.

Running cold water over the affected area relieves itching and burning of ivy poisoning.

If the itchy part of your body cannot fit under the tap, press a towel soaked in ice-cold water against it. The towel should be washed afterward so that it will not accidentally spread the poison to other areas of your skin.

There are also many commercial preparations that relieve the discomfort of ivy poisoning. A standard remedy, recommended by many dermatologists (skin doctors), is calamine lotion or ointment. This dries to

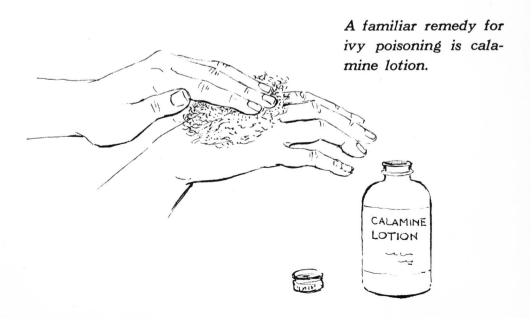

A familiar remedy for ivy poisoning is calamine lotion.

form a protective coating over the rash and helps to keep it from spreading. At the same time, it soothes the itching.

Some calamine lotions and ointments also contain antihistamines. Antihistamines are chemicals that fight allergic reactions such as ivy poisoning. Many doctors believe that antihistamines make the lotion or ointment more effective in soothing the itch.

Ordinary rubbing alcohol applied to the affected area usually relieves the itching for several hours. Be sure to pat the alcohol dry with absorbent cotton or paper tissue to avoid spreading the poison.

A time-tested remedy is a paste of baking soda and water applied to the affected area. A solution of baking soda or Epsom salt also helps to relieve the itching and discomfort. The solution should be made with one or two heaping teaspoons-

56

ful of baking soda or Epsom salts to a measuring cup of water. Apply it by holding a pad of gauze or cotton soaked in the solution on the affected area.

Whichever treatment you use to relieve the itching, repeat it every few hours until the ivy poisoning has cleared up.

Here are a few don'ts.

Don't scratch if you can possibly help it. Scratching can spread the rash by spreading traces of the poison that remain on your skin. It can also make the rash worse by irritating your skin. And, if the scratching should break the skin, bacteria may get in and cause infection.

If the itch is so bad that you feel you must scratch, some experts recommend scratching gently around the edges of the itchy area. If you do this, be careful not to touch the rash itself. If you can't help scratching the whole area, do it through a layer of clothing, such as your shirt, pants, socks, or pajamas.

Don't use your bare fingers for scratching. If you do, you will get a trace of poison on them and transfer it to other parts of your body when you touch them. In this way you can keep a case of ivy poisoning going for weeks.

Don't take baths. As you lie in the tub, some of the poison from the affected area may settle on new areas of your skin, causing the rash to spread. Showers are fine, though, because any traces of the poison picked up by the water are rinsed away. After your shower, *don't rub the affected area dry.* Instead, pat it gently and carefully with a separate towel from the one you use for drying the rest of your body.

Don't use grease or oil of any kind on

your rash. It will dissolve the poison and spread wherever it touches your skin.

Remember that different people react very differently to treatment. Therefore, a treatment that works for one person may not be helpful to another.

Once again, if you have a bad case of ivy poisoning, or if your eyes are affected— SEE A DOCTOR AT ONCE!

10

Can You Be Immunized Against Poison Ivy?

Polio vaccine immunizes you against that disease; that is, it prevents you from getting it. Doctors have also found ways to immunize people against many allergies, such as hay fever. But they have not had much success in immunizing people against poison ivy.

Extracts of the poison have been developed so that they can be taken by mouth or by injection. However, these immunizing preparations are not effective for all people. Doctors advise people who are highly sensitive to poison ivy not to use them, as they may cause the patient to break out with the symptoms of ivy poisoning.

For best results, immunizing preparations should be taken well before the poison-ivy season, so that the body has plenty of time to build up immunity. Otherwise, there is a chance that you will make yourself more sensitive. Some people who have taken antipoison-ivy shots or pills and been exposed soon afterward have gotten very severe cases of ivy poisoning. *Do not try any immunizing treatment without first checking with a doctor.*

Have you heard that eating poison ivy will make you immune? *It's not true. Don't try it!* Many children have gotten terribly sick from eating poison ivy. They have suffered diarrhea, vomiting, fever, and sometimes convulsions. Some have even died.

There are stories that hundreds of years ago, Indians used to gain immunity by eating small amounts of poison ivy. But we don't know whether or not it really worked. Doctors today warn very strongly against trying such a "treatment." The risks are too great.

Country people used to say that anyone who drank milk from cows or goats that grazed on poison ivy would be safe from ivy poisoning for that year. However, nobody seems to have done any scientific experiments to learn how much truth there is in this belief.

11

How to Get Rid
of Poison Ivy

The most convenient way of killing off poison ivy is to spray it with a chemical weed-killer, or herbicide. However, weed-killers are poisonous to people as well as to plants, and children should definitely not use them.

Perhaps one of the adults in your family would prefer to get rid of the poison ivy quickly with a chemical herbicide spray. Weed-killer sprays are sold in garden-supply stores and most hardware stores. Whoever uses the spray should carefully follow the instructions on the can. While working, he or she should wear protective clothing and gloves to keep the spray from getting on the skin. Above all, be careful not to breathe the spray. *Don't spray on a windy day.* The wind might blow the spray onto other people or onto nearby plants that you don't want to kill.

But there are other methods that are not dangerous to human beings or nearby plants. One of them doesn't need chemicals at all.

Poison ivy, like all green plants, must have light to survive. It needs the light to manufacture food by means of photosynthesis. By making use of this fact, you can kill off a small patch of poison ivy with little work or risk of exposure to the poison. You can starve the plants to death by cutting off their light supply.

Here is what to do: Cover the poison ivy with tar paper, black plastic sheeting, or a good, thick layer of newspaper, and hold the edges down with dirt, stones, or any other weight. In a month or two, the poison ivy, unable to create food by photosynthesis, should be dead. If it isn't, put the covering on for a few more weeks. If people or pets make holes in the covering, put something over the holes to keep light out.

This method must be used during the growing season. It will not work in winter, when the plants are dormant (inactive).

Before modern chemical weed-killers were developed, the U.S. Department of Agriculture recommended using brine to kill poison ivy. This treatment works more slowly than chemical weed-killers, but it has

Covering poison ivy plants with a thick layer of newspaper kills them by depriving them of sunlight. These young people are taking no chances. Note their protective clothing.

the advantage of not being harmful to people, pets, or wildlife.

To make the brine, dissolve three pounds of salt in a gallon of water. You can use table salt, but rock salt, which you can buy at hardware stores, is cheaper.

Once a week, spray the brine mixture on the leaves of the poison ivy until no new leaves grow back. Although poison ivy can stand exposure to sea water, this brine is too strong for the plant to survive for a long time.

The poison-ivy vines can also be cut off at ground level, using a scythe or a long-handled pruning shears. (This should only be done by an adult.) Then the ground should be soaked with the brine mixture once a week until the poison ivy shows no more signs of life.

Unfortunately, either one of the brine

treatments will kill not only the poison ivy, but practically all other plants growing nearby. However, you and your family may feel that it's worth it to get rid of the poison ivy.

Another treatment is to dust the ground around the poison-ivy plants with powdered borax, using one pound for every 27 square feet of soil. At this rate, a pound of borax will treat an area of 9 x 3 feet.

Like the brine, the borax treatment is practically guaranteed to kill off whatever else is growing along with the poison ivy. Brine and borax both poison the soil so that nothing will grow. Fortunately, neither of them will poison the soil permanently. In a year or two, the rain will wash enough of the brine or the borax out of the soil so that plants can grow again.

If you are not highly susceptible to ivy poisoning, an effective way to get rid of the unwelcome plant is to pull it up by the roots. With this method, there is no danger of killing nearby plants, and you do not have to work with dangerous chemicals. *But be sure to wear plenty of protective clothing!* Long pants, a long-sleeved shirt, *and especially gloves* are essential. It is best to take these precautions even if you are immune to poison ivy. Because body chemistry is very complex, you may suddenly find that you have lost your immunity and now have a case of ivy poisoning. Of course, the gloves and clothing should be washed afterward.

Try to pull up poison-ivy plants when the ground is wet and soft. They come up more easily than when the ground is dry and hard.

Pulling is most effective with young poison-ivy plants. Old plants have developed large, strong root systems that are almost

Pulling up poison ivy by the roots is a quick way of getting rid of the unwelcome plant. It is best to let an adult or a teen-ager do this job.

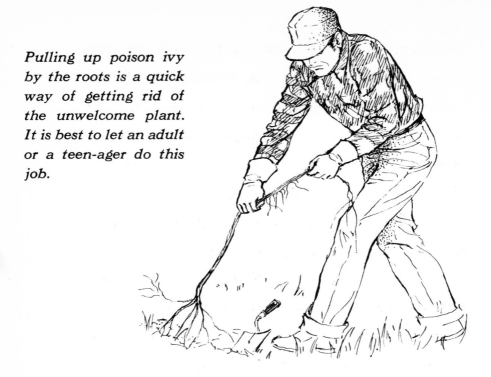

impossible to pull out entirely.

A slow, steady pull works better than a violent tug, which is likely to break the roots off in the ground. If parts of the roots are left, they will send up new leaves. However, these can be pulled up or sprayed later.

Poison ivy growing in a lawn or a field can be killed by mowing it off close to the ground. The roots will send up new leaves, but as you keep mowing them off you will notice that the new leaves are smaller and less healthy-looking. The roots are being weakened. Eventually they will starve and die.

After you have gone to the trouble of cleaning out your poison ivy, you may find it growing back the following year. The new plants may be offshoots from the spreading roots of nearby poison-ivy plants. Or they may have sprouted from seeds dropped by birds that have eaten poison-ivy berries.

Don't be discouraged. Get rid of the new poison-ivy plants as soon as you discover them. It is much easier to destroy a few new plants each year than to struggle with a thick growth of plants that have dug in their roots and gotten a strong foothold.

12
Poison Oak and Poison Sumac

Two troublesome relatives of poison ivy are poison oak and poison sumac. Both of them contain the same kind of oily, poisonous substance as poison ivy.

Despite its name, poison oak is not related to the oak trees at all. It belongs to the same plant family as poison ivy. It got its name because its leaves often look similar to oak leaves. Poison oak grows along the West Coast and in the eastern part of the United States, as far north as the middle of New Jersey.

72

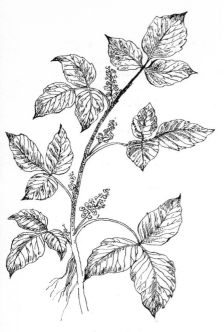

Poison Ivy

Poison Oak

Poison Sumac

Can you see the differences between poison ivy and its two troublesome relatives?

Poison oak usually grows like a bush or a shrub with many stems. Sometimes it may look like a small tree. It seldom grows more than a few feet tall, but poison oak may climb up a tree or a telephone pole.

Like poison ivy, poison oak's leaves grow in threes. The leaves, which are dark green on top and light underneath, often have a thick, leathery appearance. In the fall, they turn dark red before dropping from the plant. Poison oak also bears whitish berries like those of poison ivy.

Poison oak is about as contagious as poison ivy and causes the same kind of reaction. It should be treated in the same way as ivy poisoning.

The Indians knew poison oak well, and they treated it with caution and respect. Some tribes believed that the plant had a mind and a soul, and that it was aware of

74

Poison oak's leaves may take several different forms. Which one do you think looks most like an oak leaf? Notice that they grow in threes, like poison ivy.

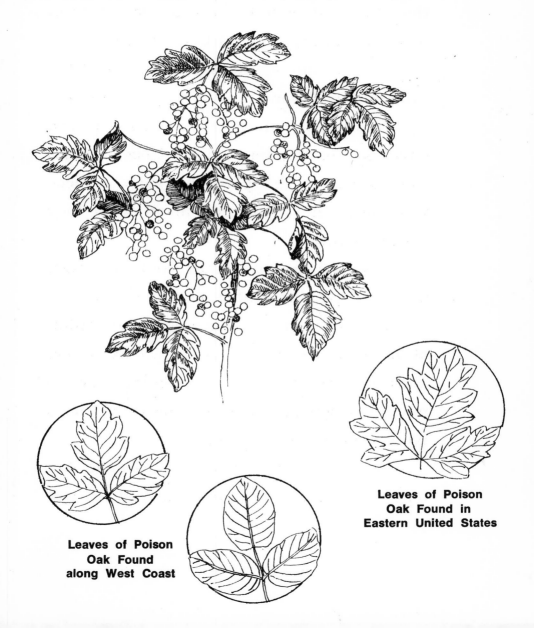

Leaves of Poison Oak Found along West Coast

Leaves of Poison Oak Found in Eastern United States

what was going on around it. Whenever these Indians were near a poison-oak plant, they called it "my friend" to keep it from becoming angry and harming them.

Poison sumac grows mostly east of the Mississippi River. In some parts of the United States, it may be known as "poison dogwood" or "poison elder." These names were given to the plant by early settlers, who were not very careful about what they called plants.

Because poison sumac contains much more poison than either poison ivy or poison oak, it is more dangerous than either of its relatives. It produces a more severe reaction, and it is more "catching." Fortunately, poison sumac is not as common as poison ivy or poison oak.

There are several kinds of sumac, but only one is poisonous. How can you tell poison sumac from the harmless kinds of sumac?

One good clue is the kind of place where the sumac is growing. The poisonous variety thrives in wet places, such as swamps, lake shores, and the banks of streams. You may find it on ground that is dry for part of the year, but almost never on permanently dry ground. So a sumac plant that is growing on a hillside is almost certainly harmless.

Most kinds of sumac, including poison sumac, are tall shrubs or small trees, from eight to twenty feet tall. (To a plant scientist, even a twenty-foot tree is "small" compared with a spreading 80-foot oak, or a 100-foot white pine.)

The narrow pointed leaves of the sumacs are another clue. The harmless sumacs have small teeth along the edges of

Poison sumac can be told from its harmless cousins by its smooth-edged leaves and greenish-white berries that hang down in loose bunches. Most harmless sumacs have tooth-edged leaves and dark red berries that grow in tight-packed, upright clusters.

their leaves, and there may be as many as twenty-five leaves on a single leaf stalk. Poison sumac has smooth-edged leaves. And there are from seven to thirteen leaves on a leaf stalk. One leaf sticks straight out from the end of the stalk, while the rest grow in pairs on opposite sides of the stalk.

The berries are another good way of telling poison sumac from its harmless relatives. Nonpoisonous kinds of sumac have dull red berries that grow in tightly packed clusters. These clusters stand upright on the plant. Poison sumac has cream-colored berries in loose clusters. And they hang down from the branches on which they grow. These cream-colored berries stay on the poison sumac plant all through the winter.

13
Poison Ivy's
Useful Relatives

At the beginning of this book, you found out that poison ivy belongs to the cashew family. There are hundreds of different plants in the cashew family, and many of them are poisonous. But, surprisingly, even some of the poisonous ones are useful to man.

The cashew tree is well known for its delicious nuts. The kernels, which are the part of the nut that we eat, are perfectly safe even when raw. However, the shells of the nuts contain a poison very much like that of poison ivy. The nuts are usually

A tasty relative of poison ivy is the cashew nut. The pear-shaped swelling above the nut is an edible fruit.

roasted before being shelled, and this destroys the poison. The poisonous oil from the shells is sometimes used to make electrical insulation for airplanes.

Although the cashew tree is native to the region around the Caribbean Sea, it was planted long ago in other parts of the world. Today India is the biggest producer of cashew nuts.

The nonpoisonous sumac trees also belong to the cashew family. Before the invention of synthetic dyes, sumac wood was used to make a bright yellow dye called fustic. The bark of sumac was also used in tanning leather. North American Indians used to make a refreshing drink from the tart, red berries of staghorn sumac.

Another useful relative of poison ivy is the Japanese lacquer tree, whose sap is used to make the famous Oriental lacquerware. When the sap is exposed to the air, it gradually dries and hardens to form a smooth, hard surface like enamel. It makes a tough but beautiful coating. Decorated bowls and boxes are probably the best-known kinds of lacquerware.

However, as the sap comes from the lacquer tree, it contains a poison like that of poison ivy, and it can cause skin irritations. Many Japanese lacquer workers suffer from this. After the lacquer dries, it is no longer poisonous.

A fourth useful member of the cashew family is the mango tree, whose fruit is an important food in tropical regions. The sweet, juicy flesh of the mango is not poisonous, but the stems of some varieties contain an irritating poison. Fortunately, man-

The Japanese lacquer tree, related to poison ivy, yields a sap that is used to make lacquerware. The sap, irritating when liquid, is harmless when dry.

goes come to market without their stems, so you don't need to worry if you handle one in a store.

Still another relative of poison ivy is the pistachio nut, a favorite of many people. The pistachio nut grows on a small tree native to southwest Asia. It has been raised by man since very ancient times. Even in Biblical times, the pistachio nut was a popular treat. The original Hebrew version of the Old Testament tells us that pistachio nuts were among the gifts that Joseph's

Although the pistachio nut is native to the Middle East, it is a popular snack in many countries. The nut and the tree it grows on are not poisonous.

brothers took to him when he became a powerful official in Egypt.

Even poison ivy had a use in Colonial times. American schoolboys sometimes marked their laundry with poison-ivy sap, since it made a permanent, inky-black stain. It is safe to guess that only boys who did not get ivy poisoning used this "ink."

14

Some Harmless "Look-Alikes" of Poison Ivy

People sometimes mistake harmless plants for poison ivy. The plant most often mistaken for the three–leaved itch-giver is probably the Virginia creeper, a handsome vine that belongs to the grape family. Like poison ivy, Virginia creeper is a climber, and the two plants often grow in the same place, sometimes even on the same tree or rock.

However, Virginia creeper is easy to tell apart from poison ivy because its leaves grow in groups of five, not three. Occasionally you may find a set of three leaves on a Virginia-creeper vine, but you will always find sets of five leaves as well. The leaves of Virginia creeper are also shaped differently from those of poison ivy.

Here are some extra clues. The fruits of Virginia creeper are small, blue berries; poison-ivy berries are grayish white. The stem of Virginia creeper does not become hairy as it grows older; the poison ivy stem does.

Because poison-ivy leaves grow in threes, some people avoid all plants with three leaves, including some that are not even vines. But not all three-leaved plants are dangerous.

Wild brambles are sprawling vines with leaves in threes. Their leaves are edged with small teeth, and their stems are thorny.

Wild strawberries are small, bushy

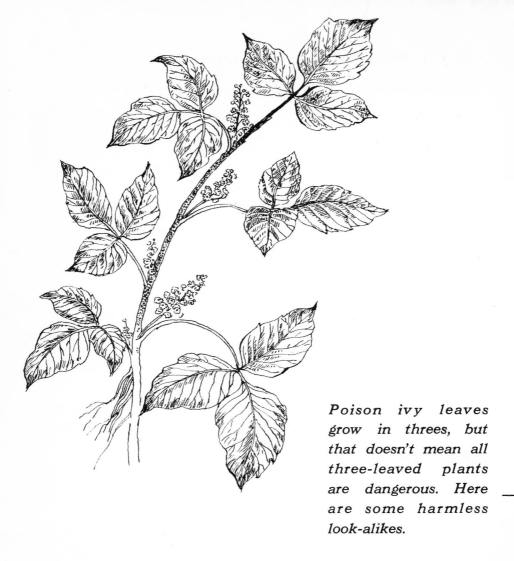

Poison ivy leaves grow in threes, but that doesn't mean all three-leaved plants are dangerous. Here are some harmless look-alikes. →

plants with leaves that grow in threes. The leaves are deeply toothed, and are very regular. Poison-ivy leaves, if they are

A shaft of sunlight falls on Virginia creeper at the edge of a woods. Note the five leaves and their characteristic shape.

This wild strawberry, growing along the edge of a garden, is perfectly safe to touch.

Jack-in-the-pulpit has a fleshy stalk and groups of three large leaves.

Ground ivy is one of the names given to this harmless three-leaved plant.

toothed, have irregular teeth. The veins in the leaves of the two plants also look very different, as you can see from the illustrations. In late spring, wild strawberries bear bright, white blossoms with yellow centers. In early summer, the red berries provide another clue that this plant is not poison ivy.

There isn't room here to list all the plants that could possibly be mistaken for poison ivy, but you don't need to make mistakes.

Look closely at the plant you suspect might be poison ivy or one of its relatives. Look for all its identifying features. Use the pictures in this book to help you decide whether a plant is dangerous or not.

Don't take chances with poison ivy, but don't let the fear of ivy poisoning keep you from enjoying the outdoors.

Glossary

Absorbent   Able to soak up liquids quickly and easily, like a sponge or a paper towel.

Allergy   A harmful reaction of the body to a substance, such as wool, or a food.

Antibody   A chemical substance produced by the body, which normally helps it to fight disease and infection.

Antihistamines   Chemicals that neutralize the harmful chemicals produced by the body's cells in an allergic reaction.

Botanist   A scientist who specializes in the study of plants.

Brine   A strong solution of salt in water; very salty water.

Dormant   Inactive, as if asleep for the winter.

Exposure   Being exposed to.

Herbicide   A chemical or mixture of chemicals that kills plants; a chemical weed-killer.

Immune   Not affected by.

Infection   What happens when bacteria, viruses, or other germs get into your body.

Microscopic   Something microscopic is so small that it can only be seen with the aid of a microscope.

Photosynthesis   The process by which plants turn the energy of sunlight into sugar and starch to use as nourishment.

Pus   The thick, yellowish-white liquid produced in infected cuts and sores, pimples, and boils. Pus consists mostly of dead bacteria and white blood cells.

Sensitive   Easily affected by; reacting strongly to.

Substance   A particular kind of material, such as steel, glass, oil, or peanut butter.

Susceptible   Easily affected by.

Symptom   An effect of disease or sickness that shows that something is wrong.

Index

A

Africa, 30
Allergic reactions, 32-33, symptoms of, 34, 35, 56
Allergies, 60
America/Americans, 9, 85
Anacardiaceae, 10
Animals, 41-42
Antibodies, 33
Antihistamines, 56
Antipoison-ivy shots, 61
Asia, 30, 84

B

Bacteria, 57
Bahamas, 30
Baking soda, as treatment, 56-57
Baths, 58
Beach, poison ivy on, 27
Bermuda, 30
Berries, poison ivy, 23, 32, 42, 71, 87; poison oak, 74; poison sumac, 79; staghorn sumac, 82; Virginia creeper, 87; wild strawberries, 90
Biblical times, 84
Blisters, 49, 51, 52, 53
Bois de puce (flea-wood), 10
Borax, 68
Botanists, 10-12, 77
Branches, poison ivy, 35

Brine, 65-66, 67, 68
Bush, poison ivy resemblance to, 16

C

Calamine lotion, 55, 56
California, 27
Canada/Canadians, 10, 28
Canals, microscopic, 39
Caribbean Sea, 81
Cashew family, 10, 12, 80; members of, 80-84
Cashew tree, description of, 80-81; location of, 81
Central America, 30
Chain reaction, 33
Chemicals, 34, 56, 64, 69
City lots, poison ivy on, 27
Climbing roots, poison ivy, 12, 15
Climbing sumac, 10
Clothing, protective, 36, 64, 69
Cold water, as treatment, 54-55
Colonists, American, 9, 85
Commercial preparations, 55
Cornell University, 35
Country people, 9, 62
Creams and lotions, 38

D

Dermatologists, 55
Dormant, 65
Drug manufacturers, 38

93

E

Egg white, 33
Egypt, 85
Epsom salt, as treatment, 56-57
Europe, 9, 30

F

Farmland, poison ivy on, 27, 30
Fences, poison ivy on, 15, 26, 30
Fields, poison ivy in, 15, 27, 30, 70-71
"Fingers three, don't touch me," 20
Flowers, poison ivy, 23, 32; jewelweed, 46; wild strawberries, 90
Folk remedy, 10
Folk rhyme, 20
Frontiersmen, 9, 47
Fustic, 82

G

Garden, poison ivy in, 30
Grape family, 86
Grease, 58-59
Guatemala, 30

H

Harvard University, 32
Hay fever, 60
Hebrew, 84
Herbicide, 63

I

Immunity, 34, 61, 62, 69
Immunization, poison ivy, 60, 61; folk stories regarding, 61-62
India, 81
Indians, North American, 47, 62, 74, 76, 82
Infection, 33
Injection, 60
Insect eggs, 22
Itching, 49, 51, 53-55, 57
Ivy poisoning, folk remedies for, 10, 47; susceptible to, 34, 36, 68; creams and lotions for, 38; getting, 39-41; prevention of, 43-47; symptoms of, 48-51, 61; duration of, 51; treatment of, 53-59; in eyes, 53, 59; 61, 62, 68, 69, 74, 90. *See also* Poison ivy

J

Japan, 30
Japanese lacquer tree, 82-83
Japanese workers, 85
Jewelweed, 46-47
Joseph, 84

L

Lacquerware, Oriental, 82-83
Lawn, poison ivy in, 30, 70-71
Leaflets, poison ivy, 21

R

Ragweed pollen, 33
Rash, 9, 32, 48, 51, 56, 57, 58, 59
Reactions. *See* Allergic reaction
Redness, 49
Rhus radicans, 12
Rhus toxicodendron, 12
Rocks, poison ivy on, 15, 26, 27
Roots, poison ivy, 32, 39, 69-70, 71
Rootlets, poison ivy, 15, 26
Rubbing alcohol, 45, 56

S

Sap, Japanese lacquer tree, 82; poison ivy, 24, 32, 33, 39, 85
Scratching, 57-58
Seeds, poison ivy, 71
Settlers, American, 47, 76
Soap, as treatment, 43-44, 45
South America, 30
Sprays, 63-64, 67
Stems, poison ivy, 15, 18, 24-26, 32, 39, 87; poison oak, 74; poison sumac, 79
Stone walls, poison ivy on, 15, 26, 30
Streaks, raised, 49
Sumac, nonpoisonous, 12, 76-77, leaves of, 77-79; wood of, 82; bark of, 82; staghorn, 82
Sunlight, 31. *See also* Photosynthesis
Susceptibility, 34, 36, 40, 41, 68

Swamps, poison ivy in, 27
Swelling, 49, 51, 53
Symptoms, ivy poisoning, 34, 48-52, 54, 61

T

Taiwan, 30
Telephone poles, poison ivy on, 15
Three-leaved ivy, 10
Treatment, ivy poisoning, 53-59
Trees, poison ivy in, 15, 26

U

United States, 28, 72, 76
U.S. Department of Agriculture, 65

V

Vaccine, 60
Veins in leaves, 90
Vines, poison ivy, 15, 18, 25, 26, 67, 87; Virginia creeper, 86; wild brambles, 87
Virginia creeper, 86-87

W

Weed-killers, 63-64, 65, 70
West Coast, 72
Wild brambles, 87
Wild strawberries, 87-90
Wilderness, poison ivy in, 27
Woods, poison ivy in, 15, 27, 30-31